THIS BOOK BELONG TO ....

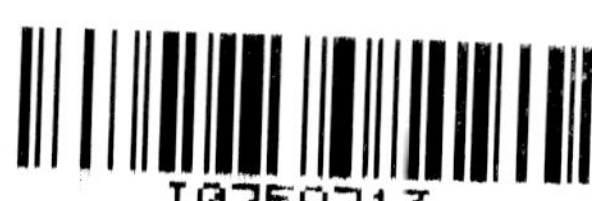

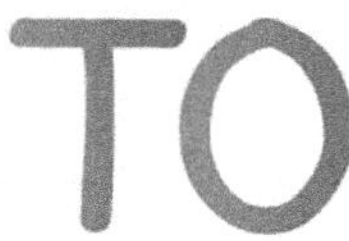

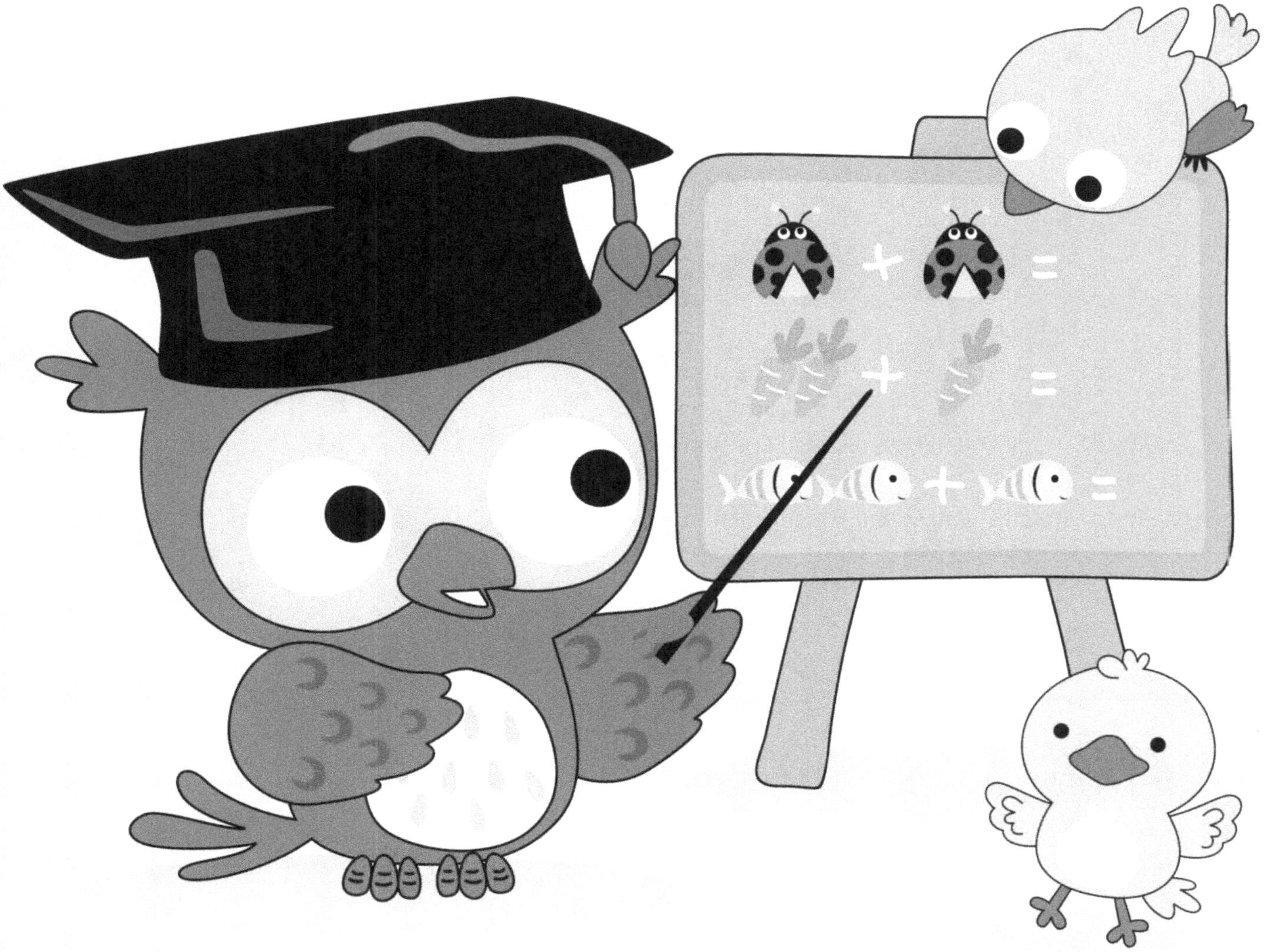

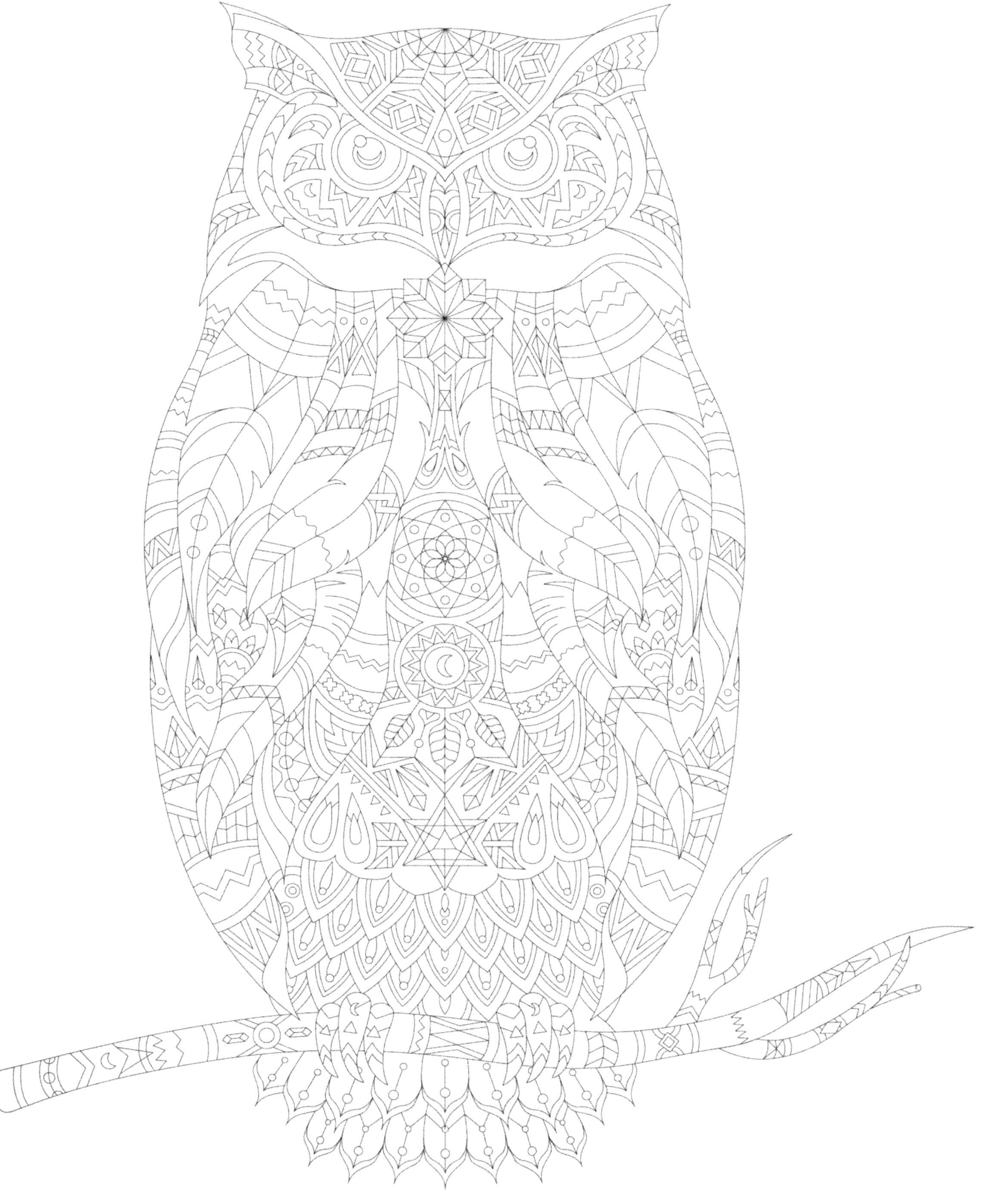

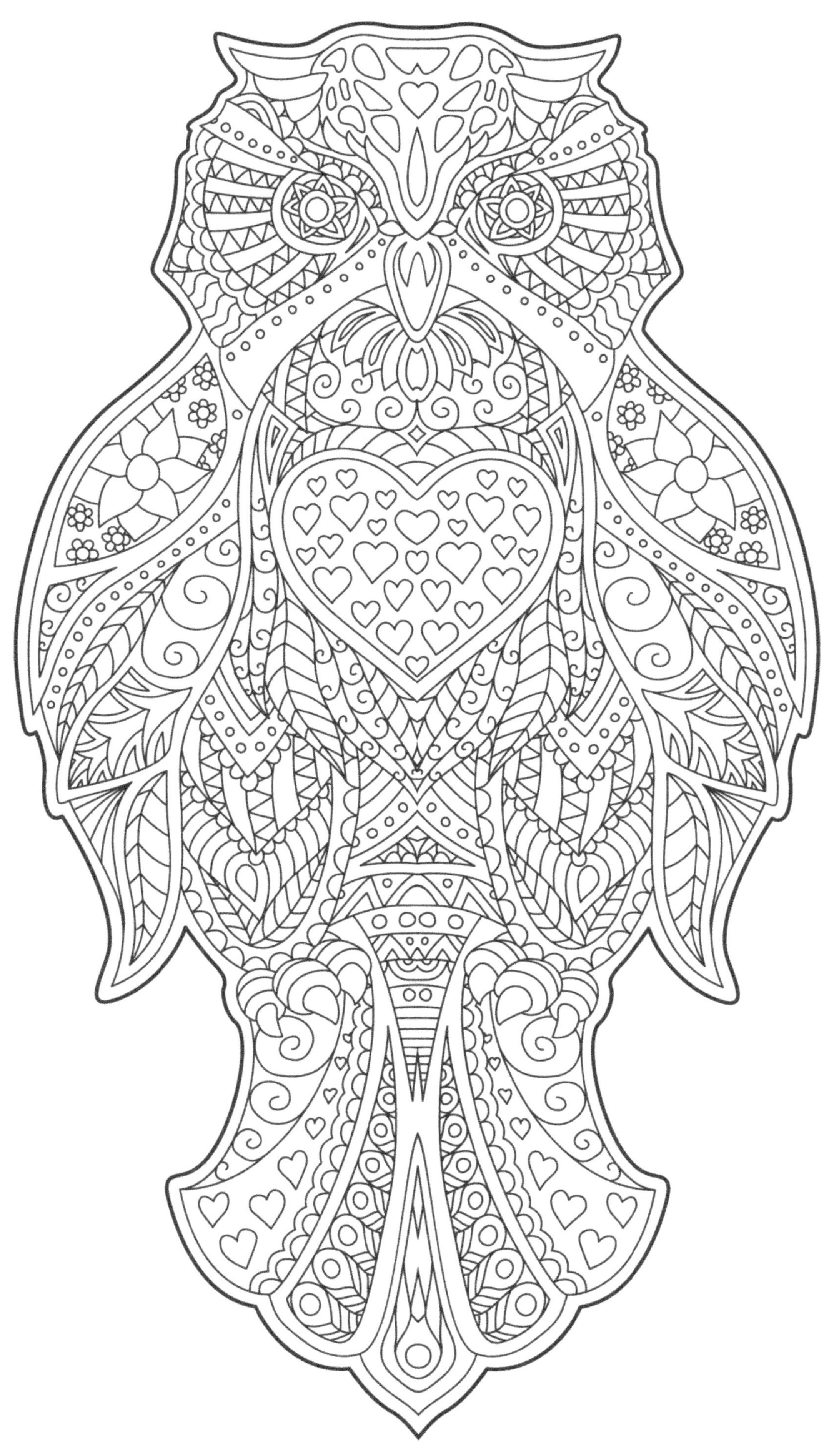

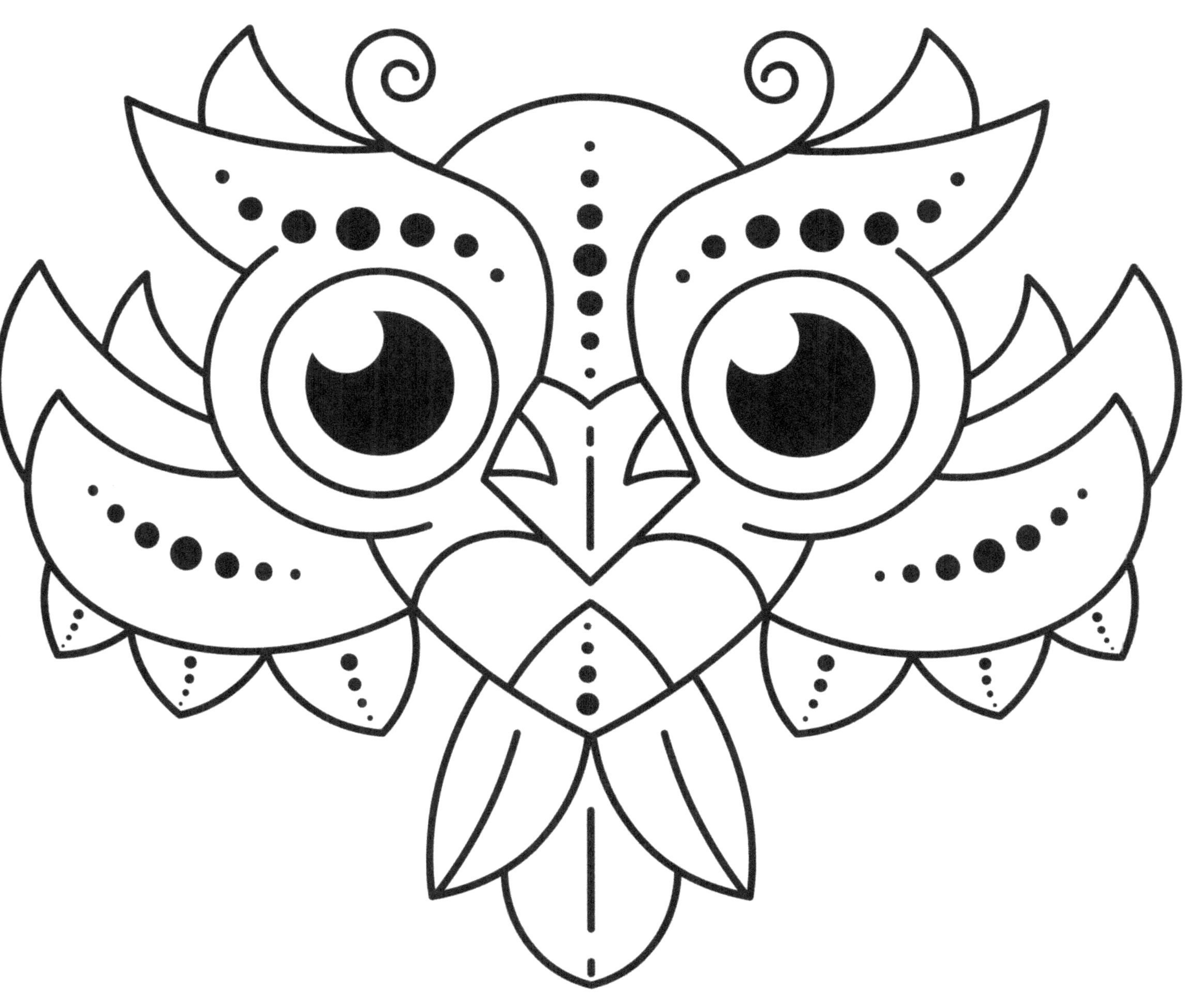

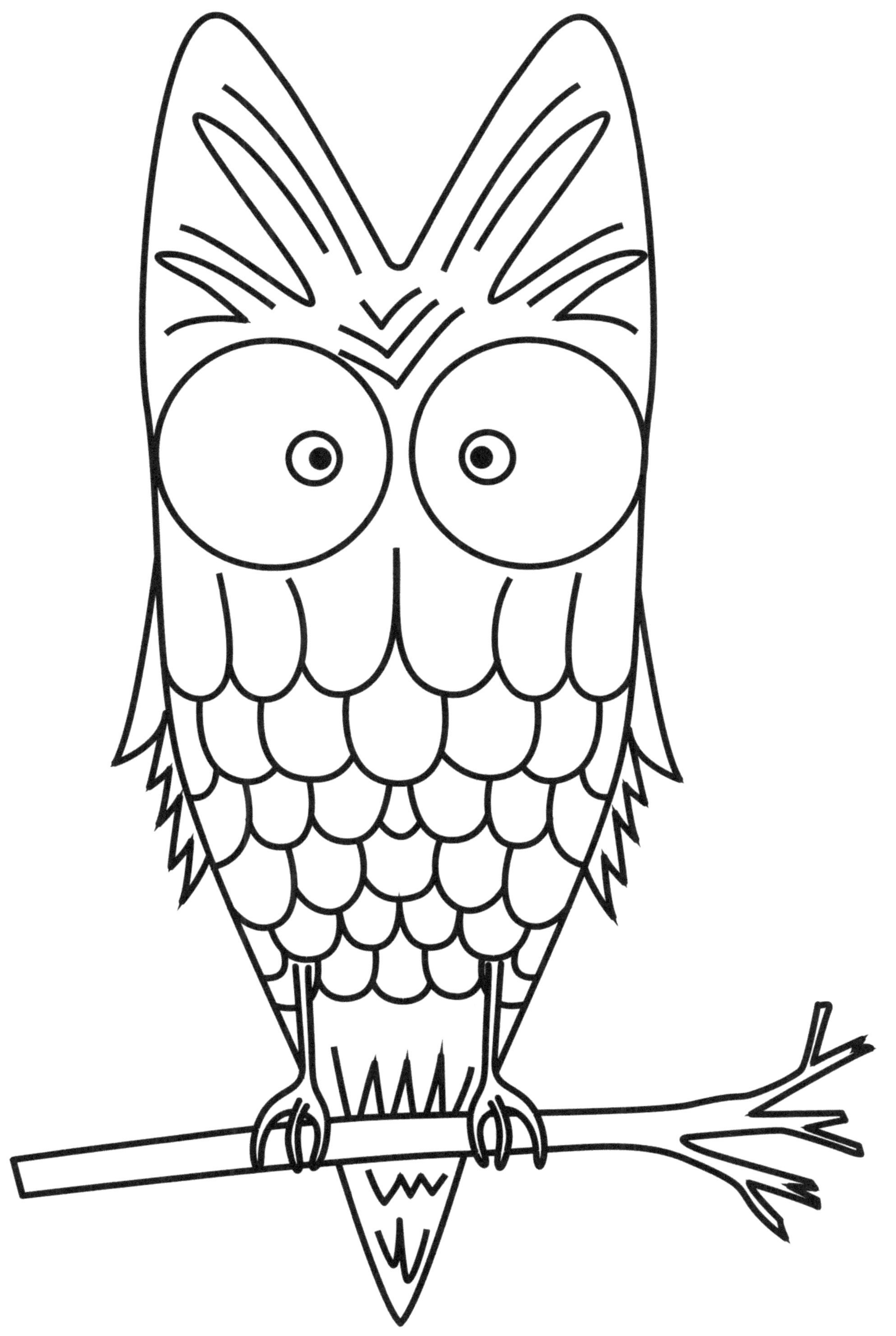

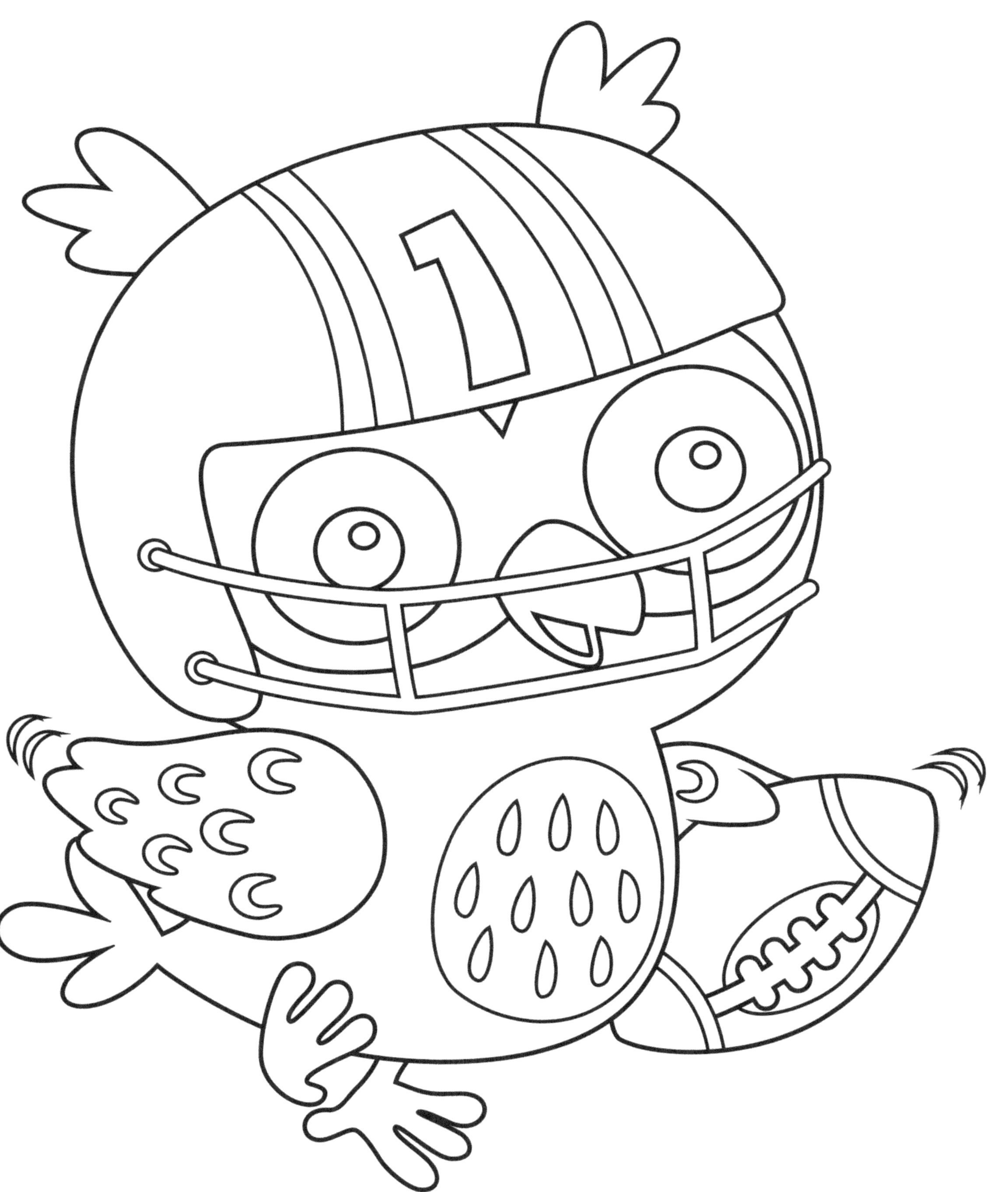

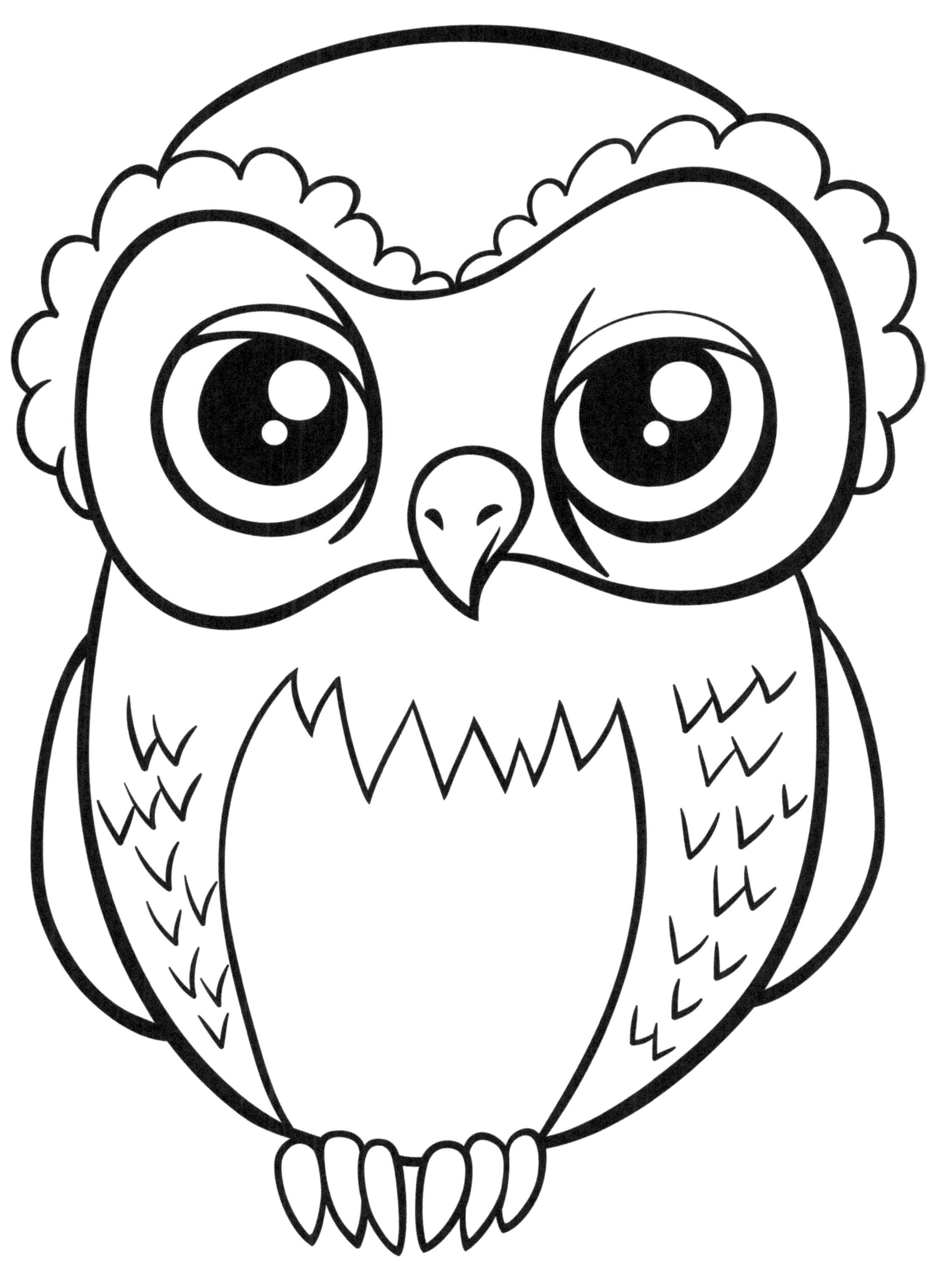

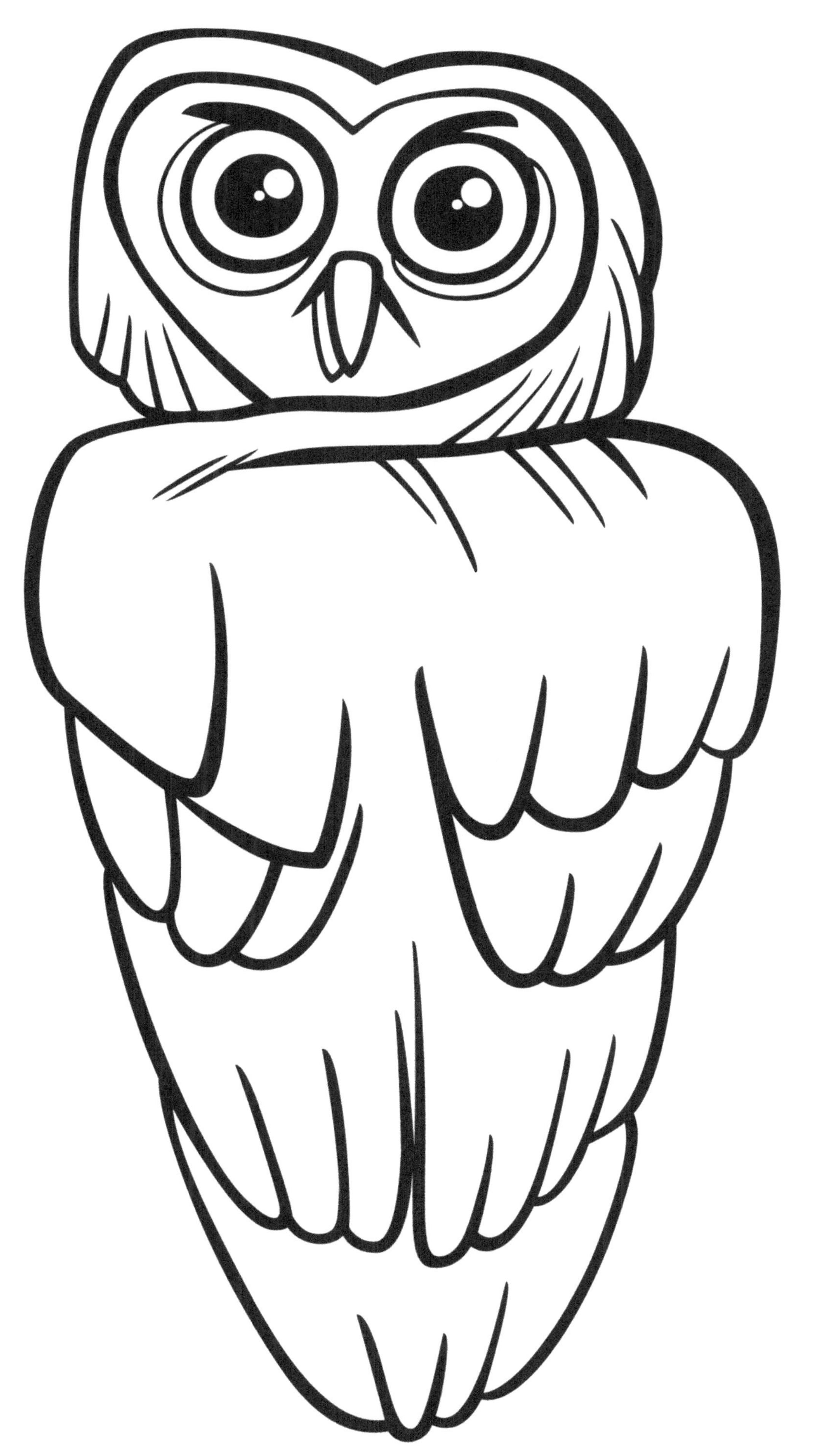

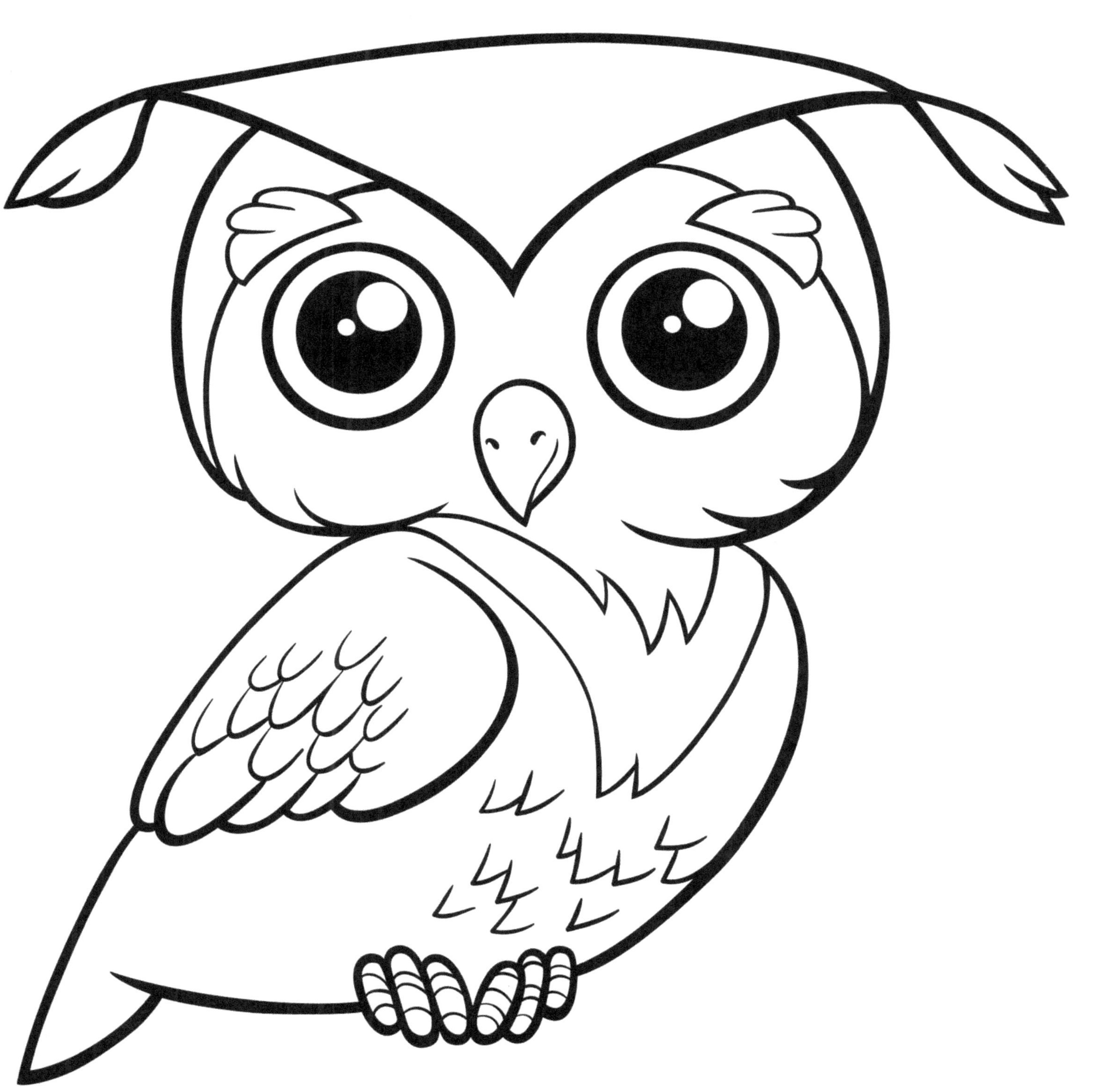

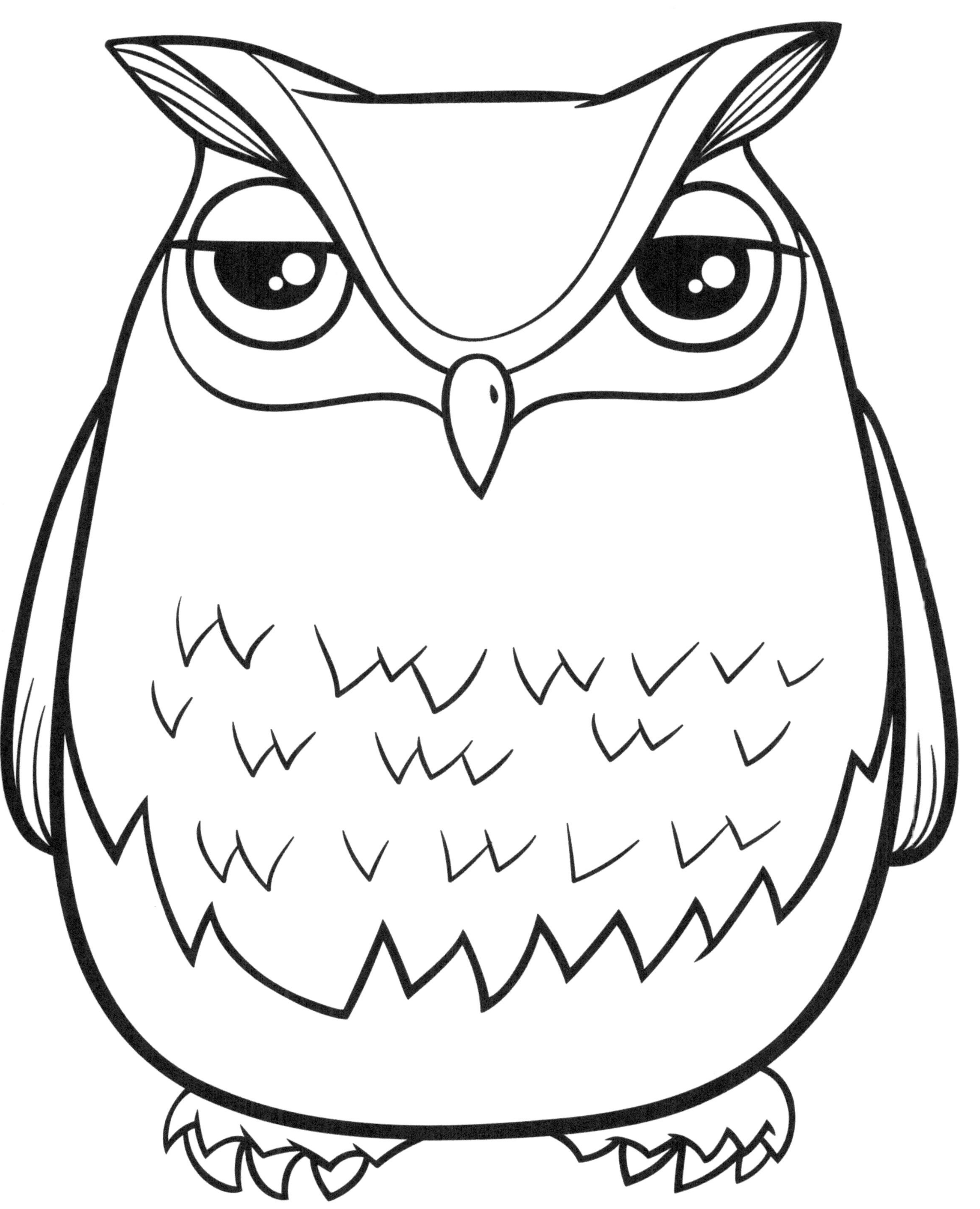

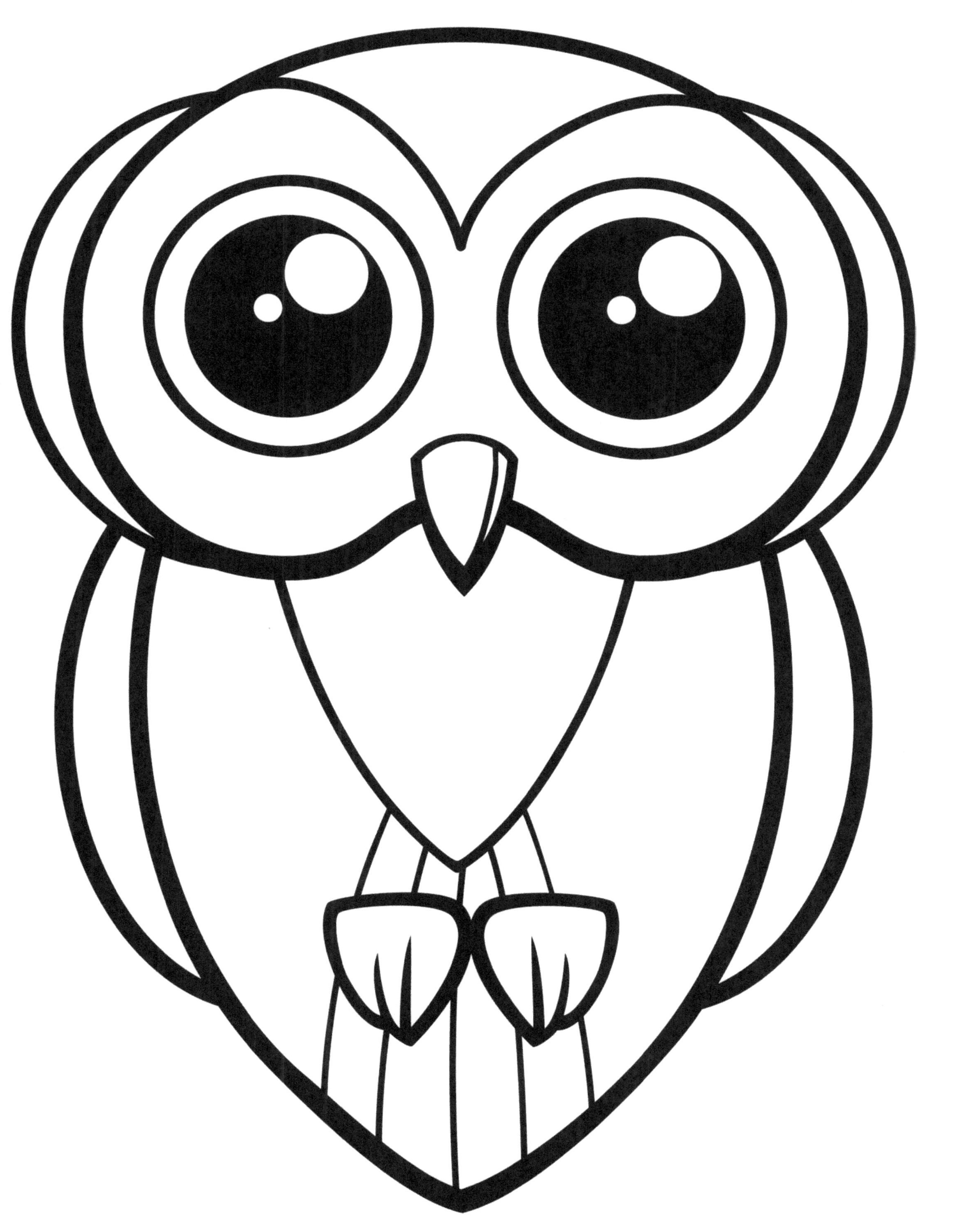

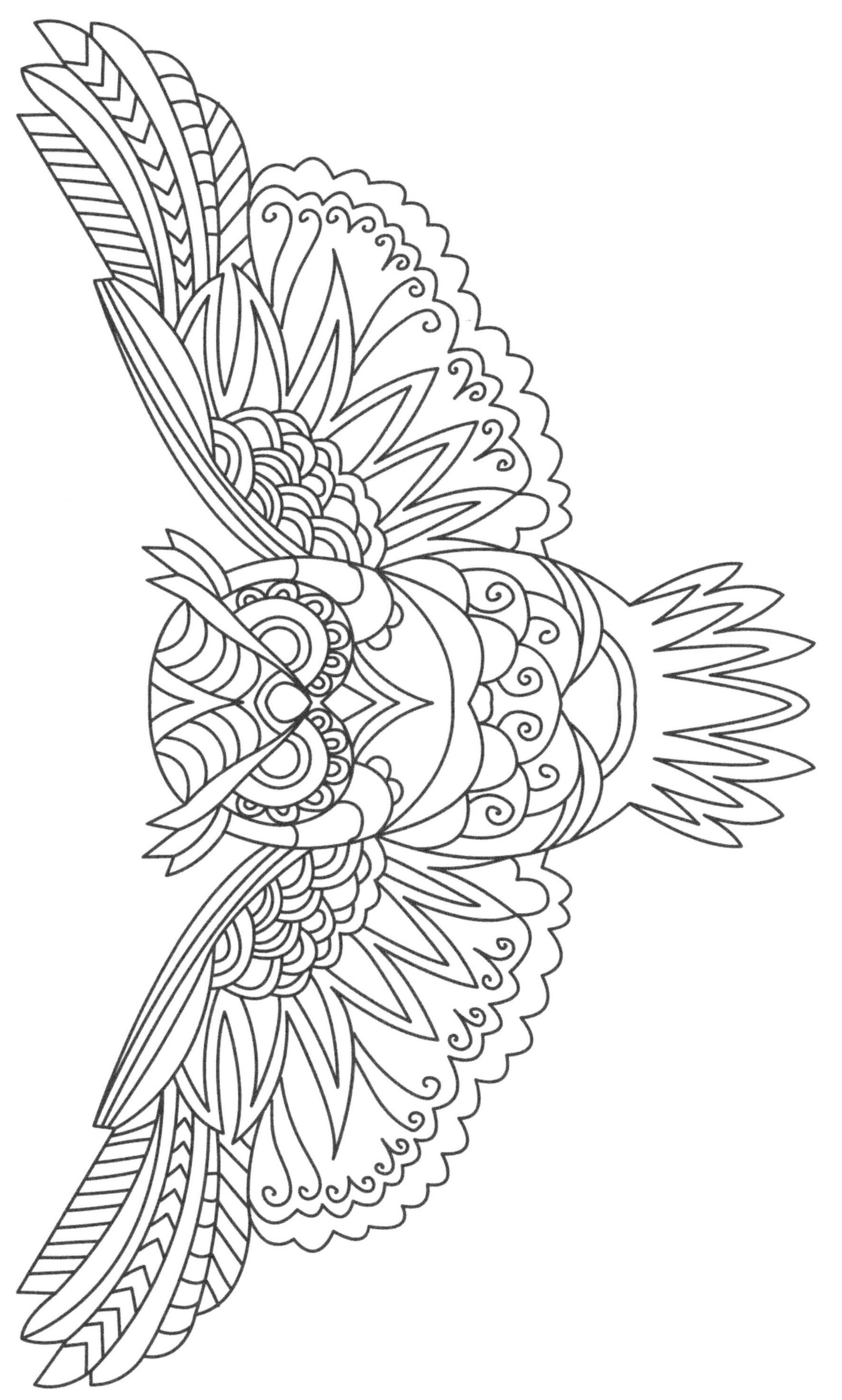

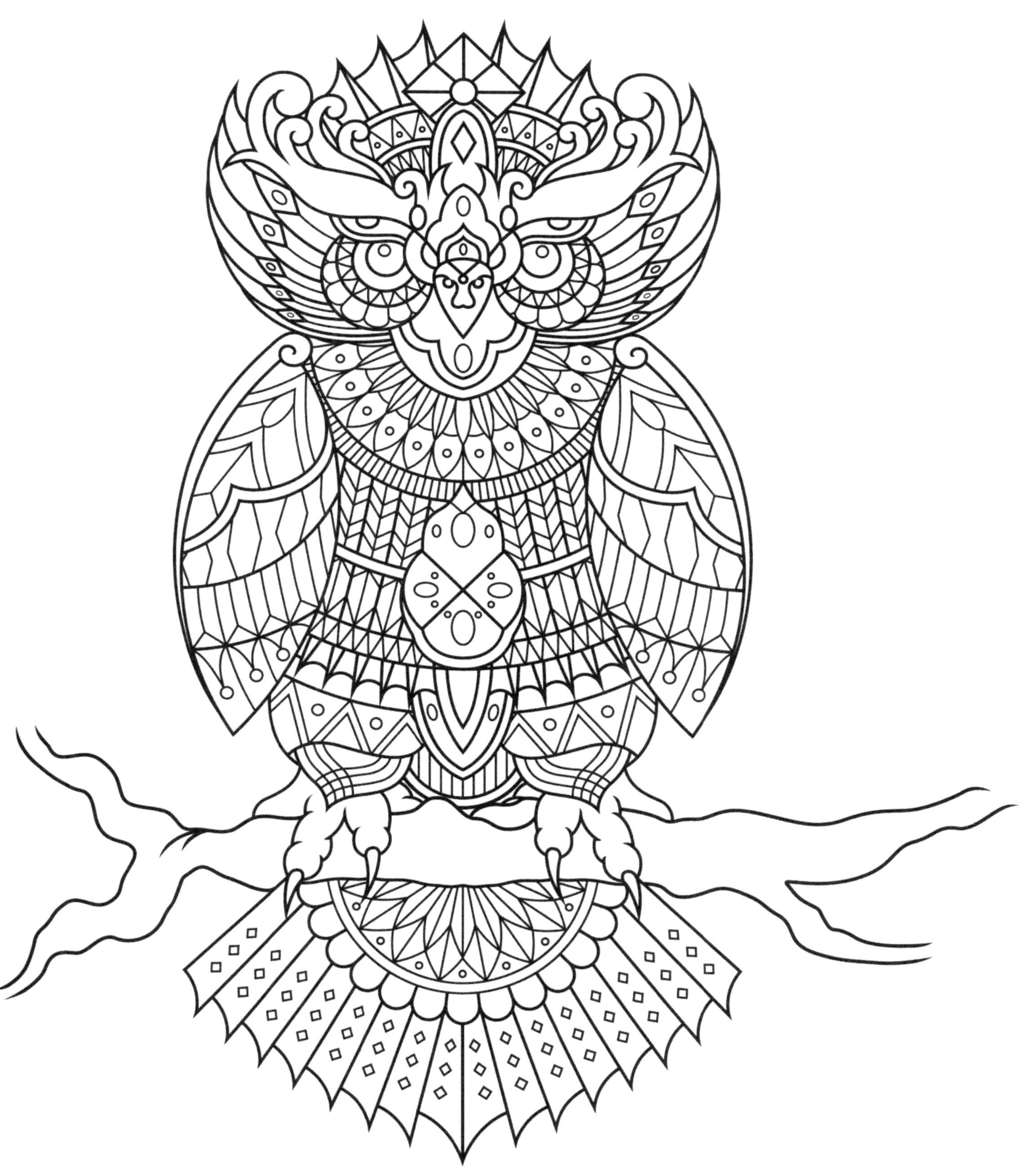

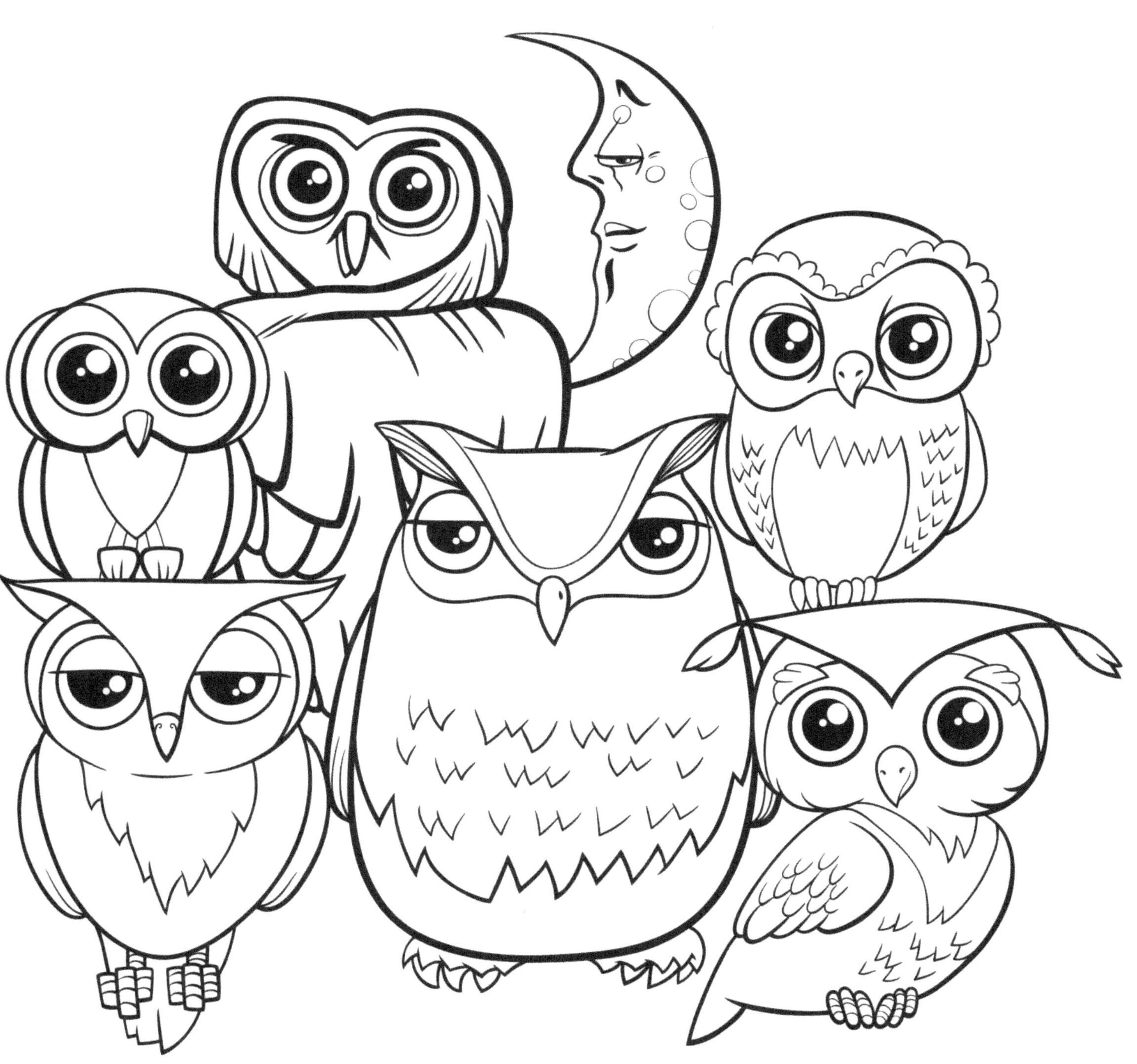

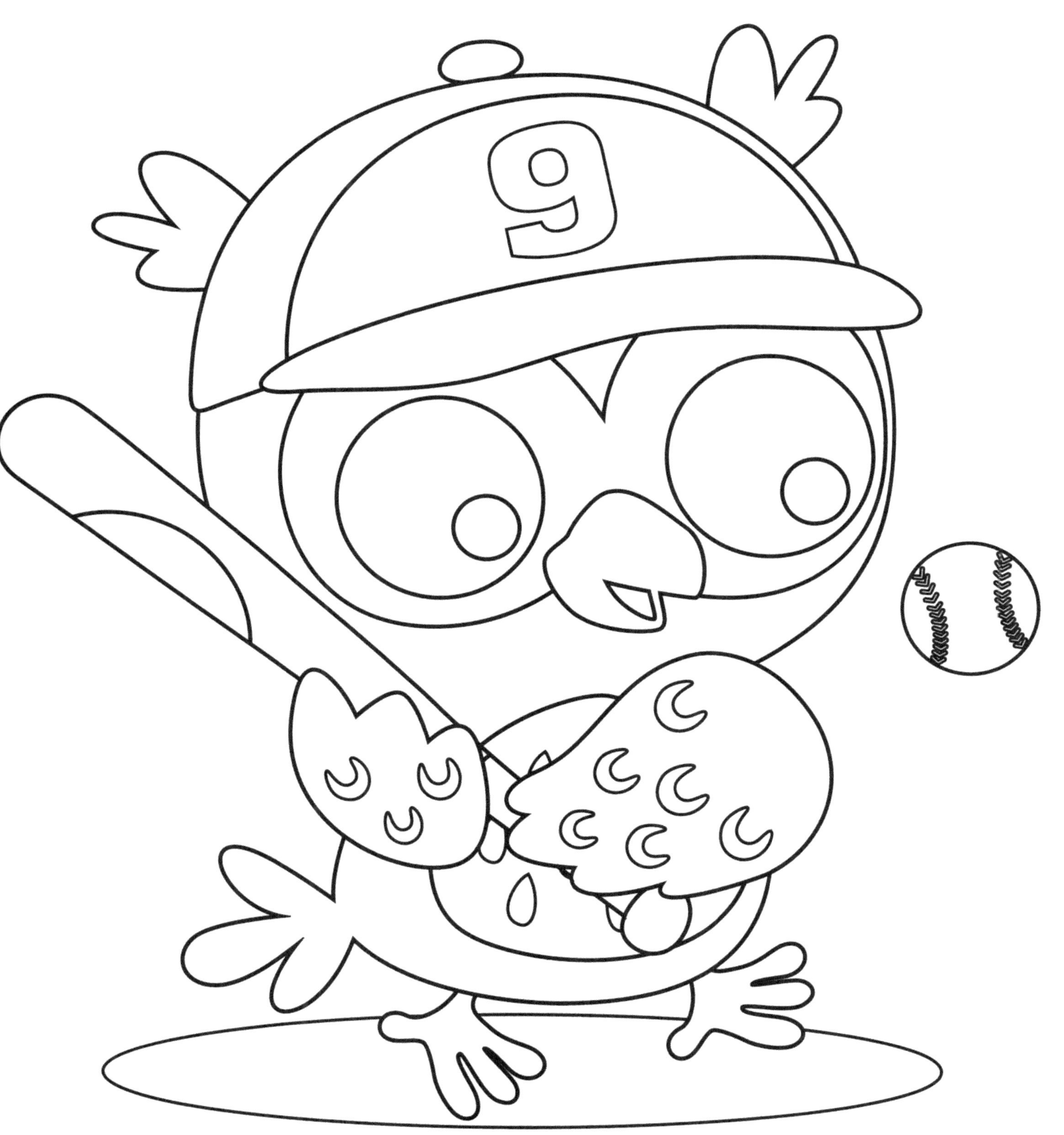

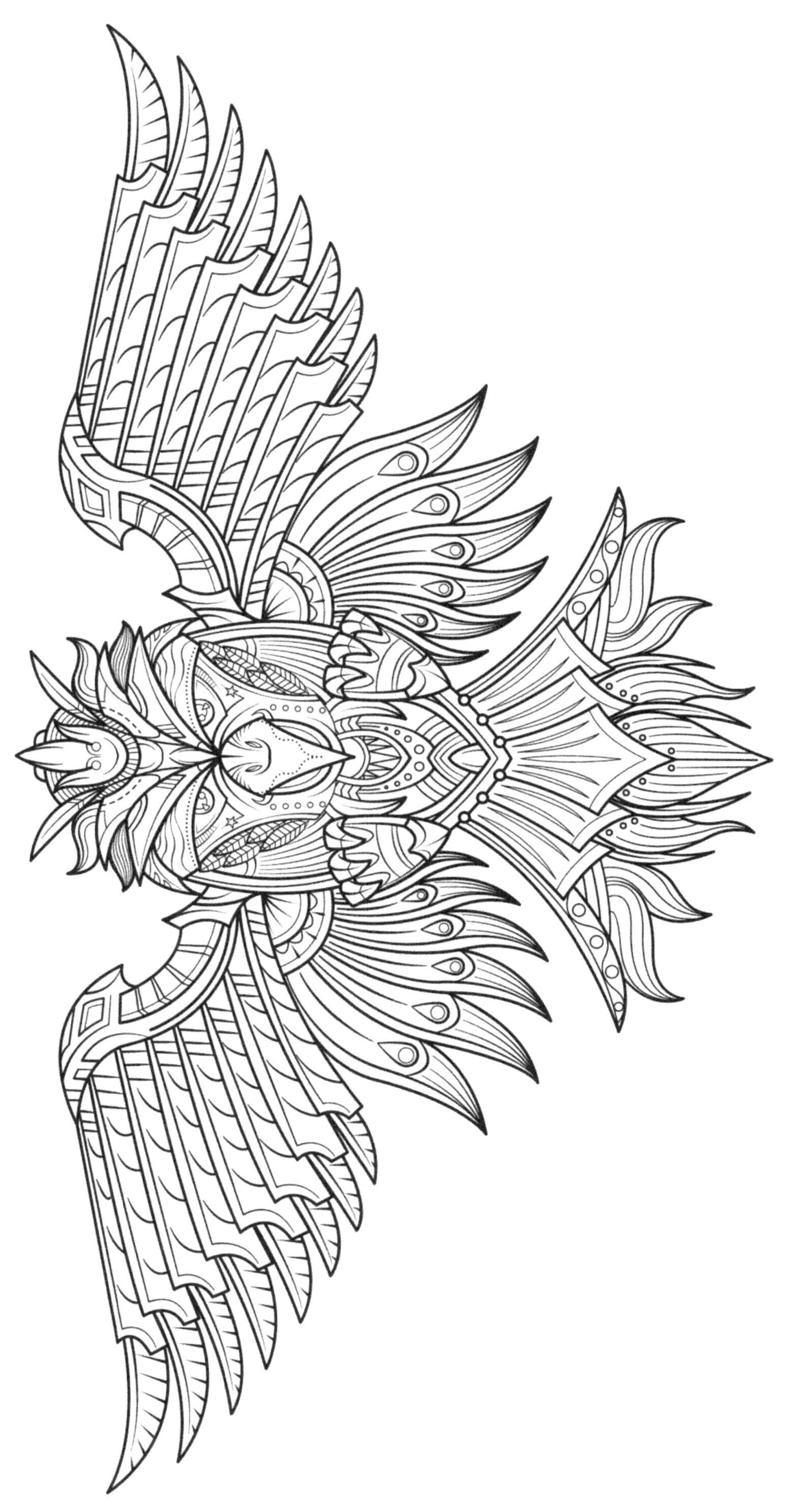

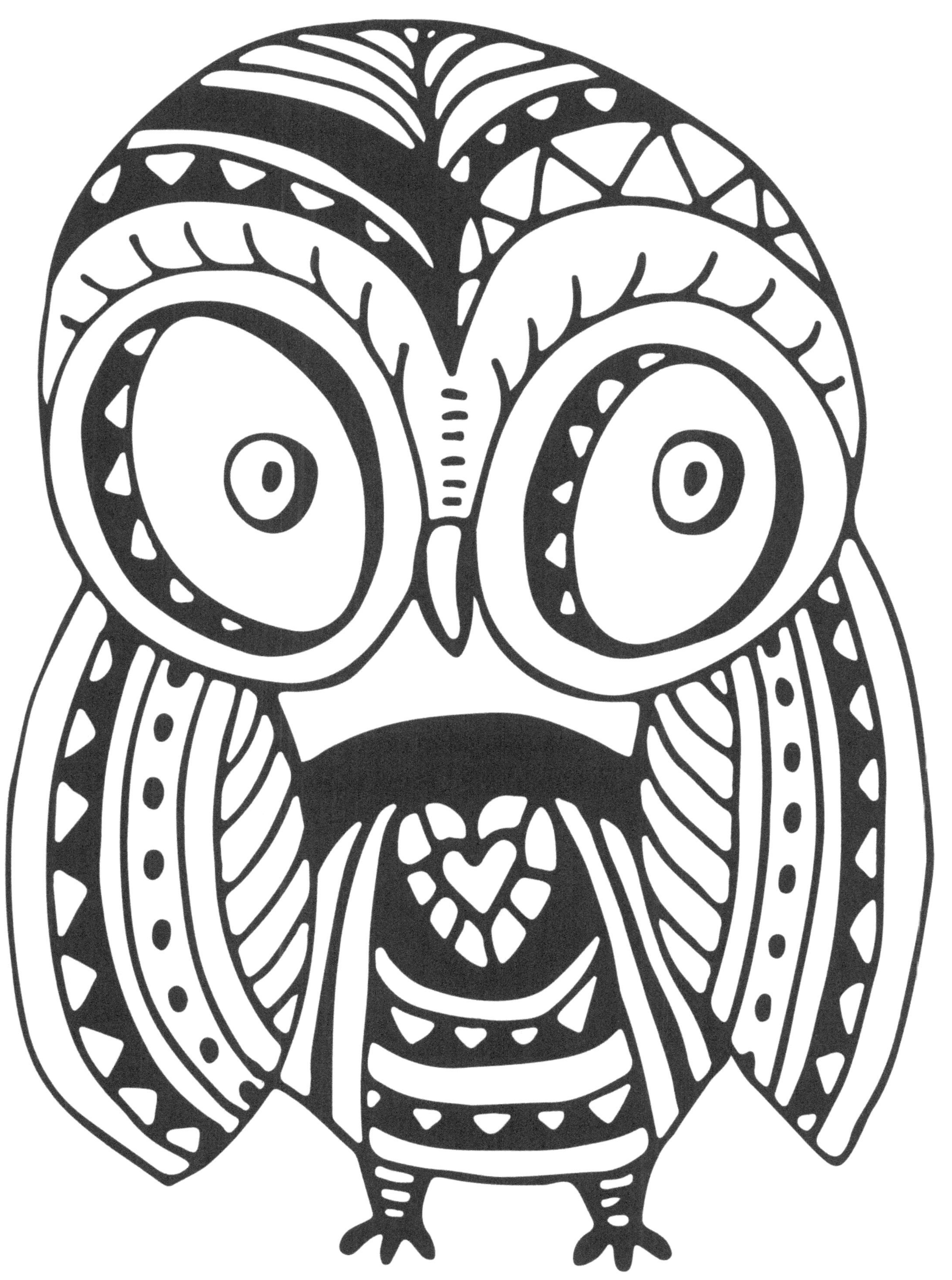

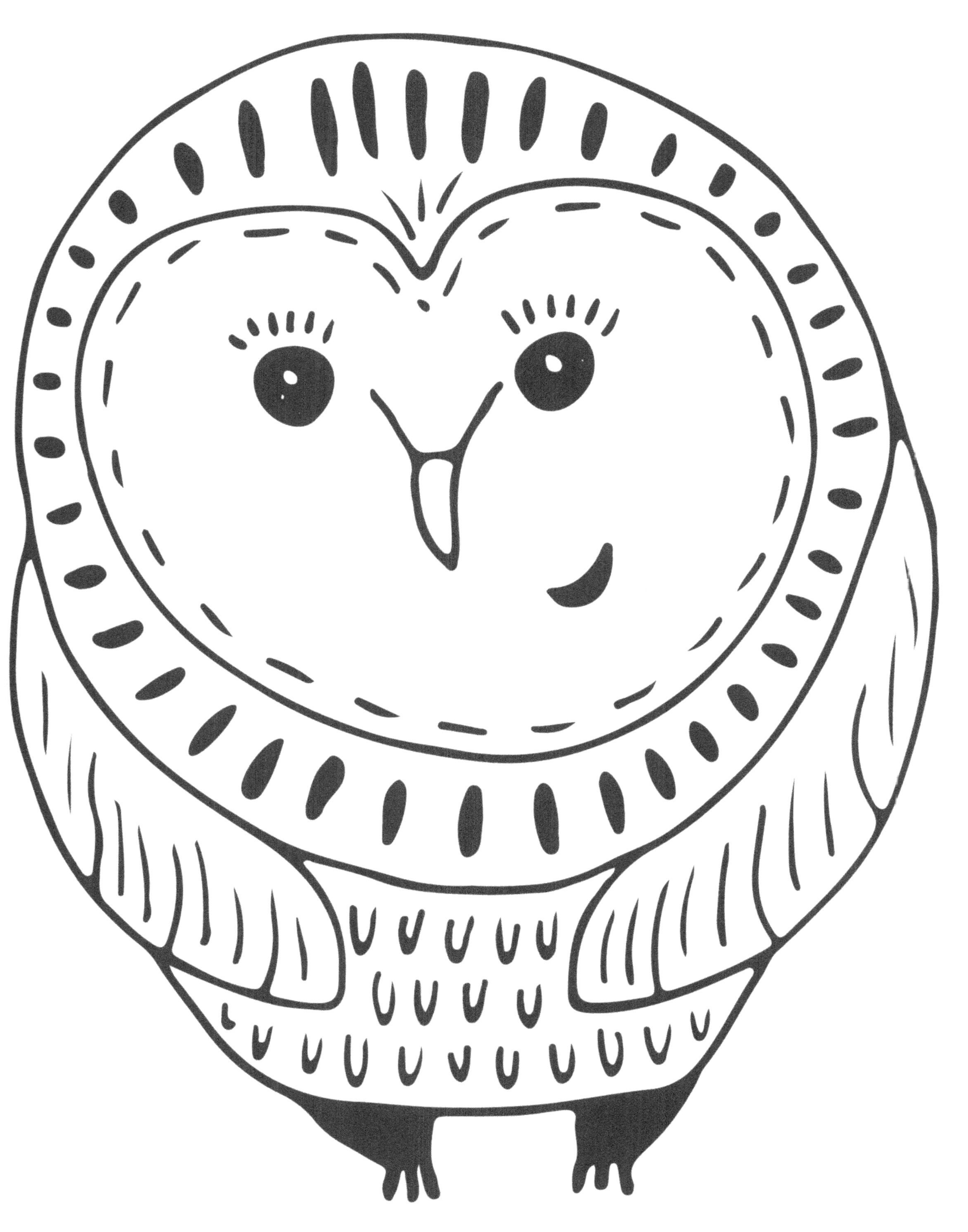

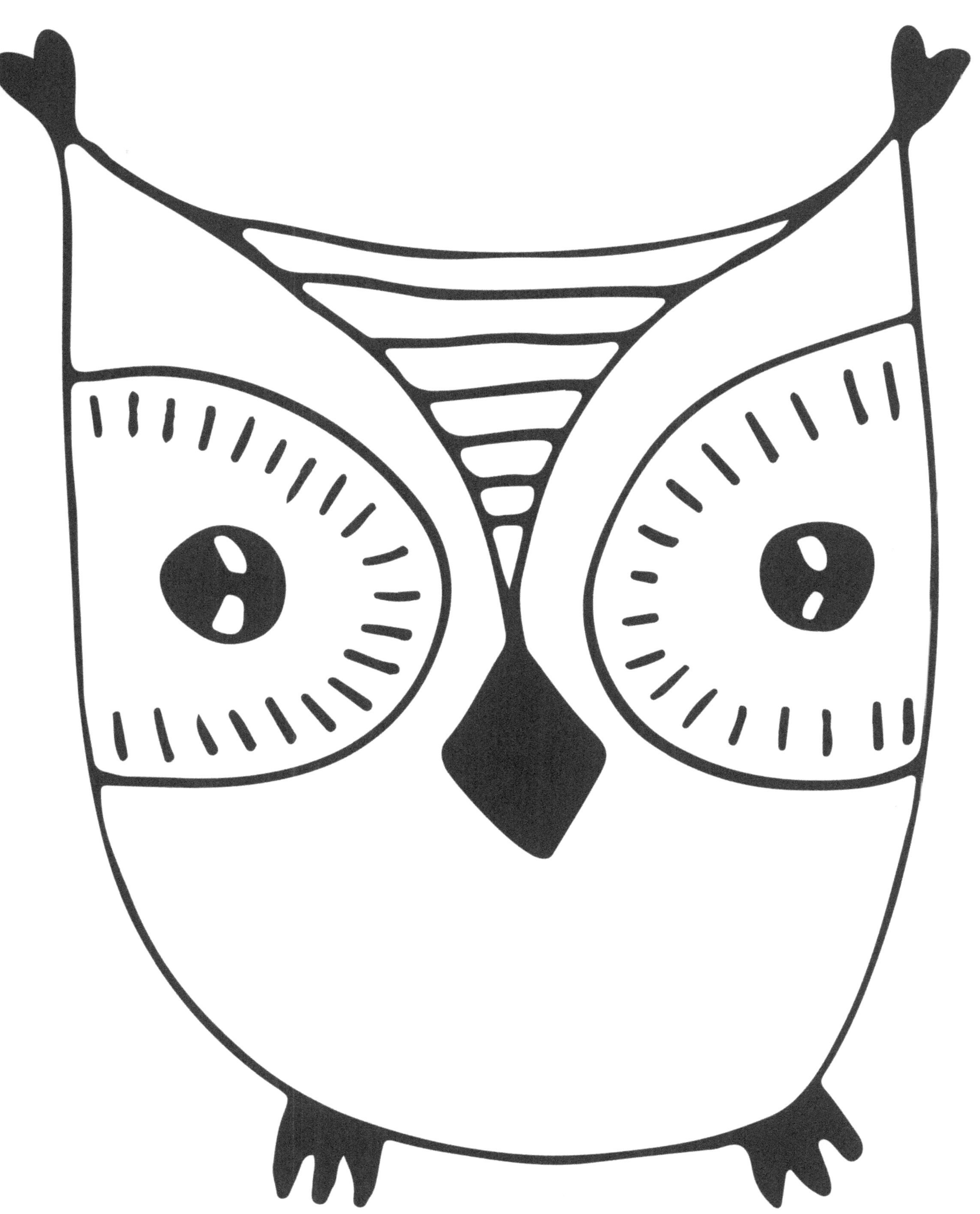

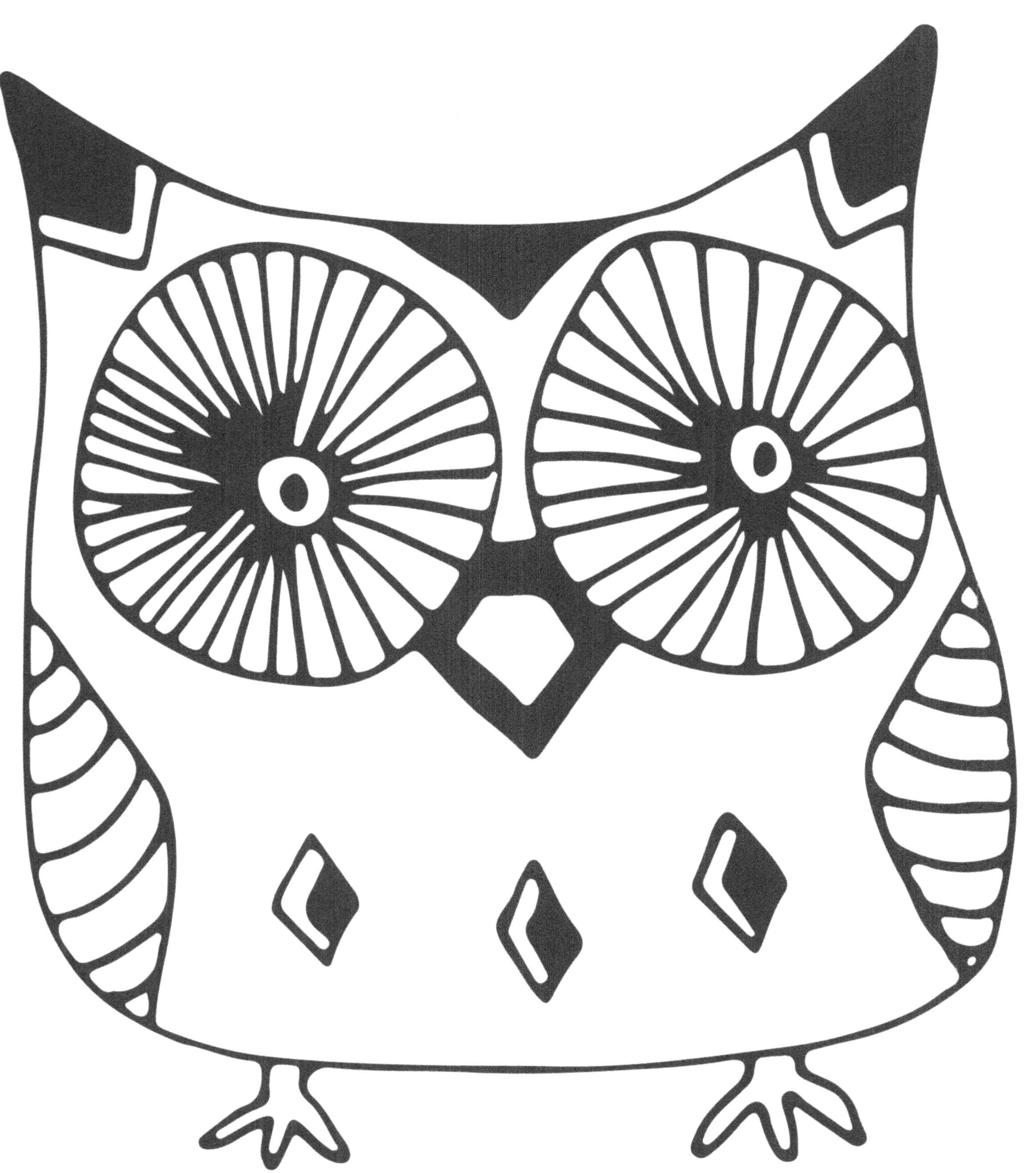

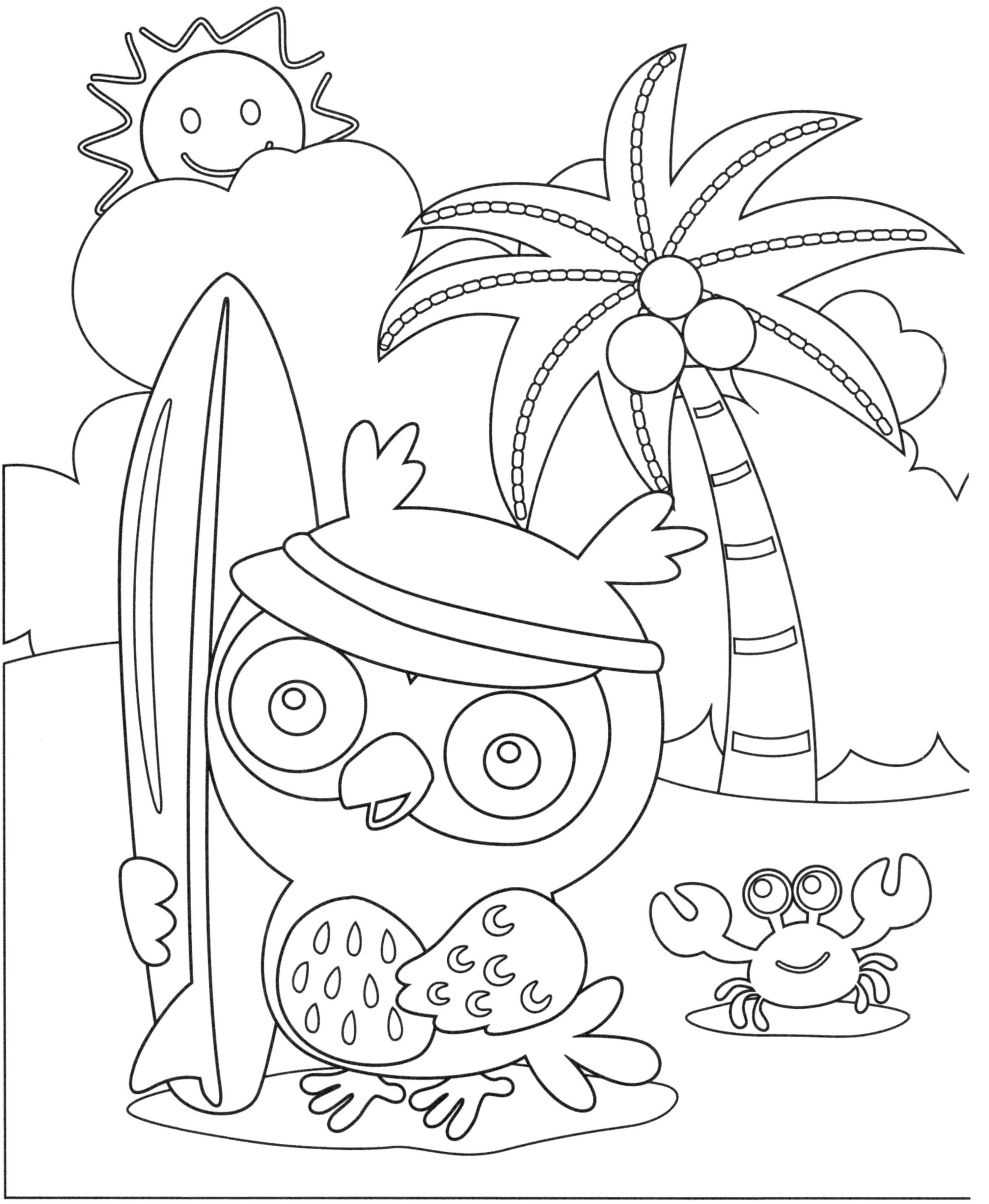

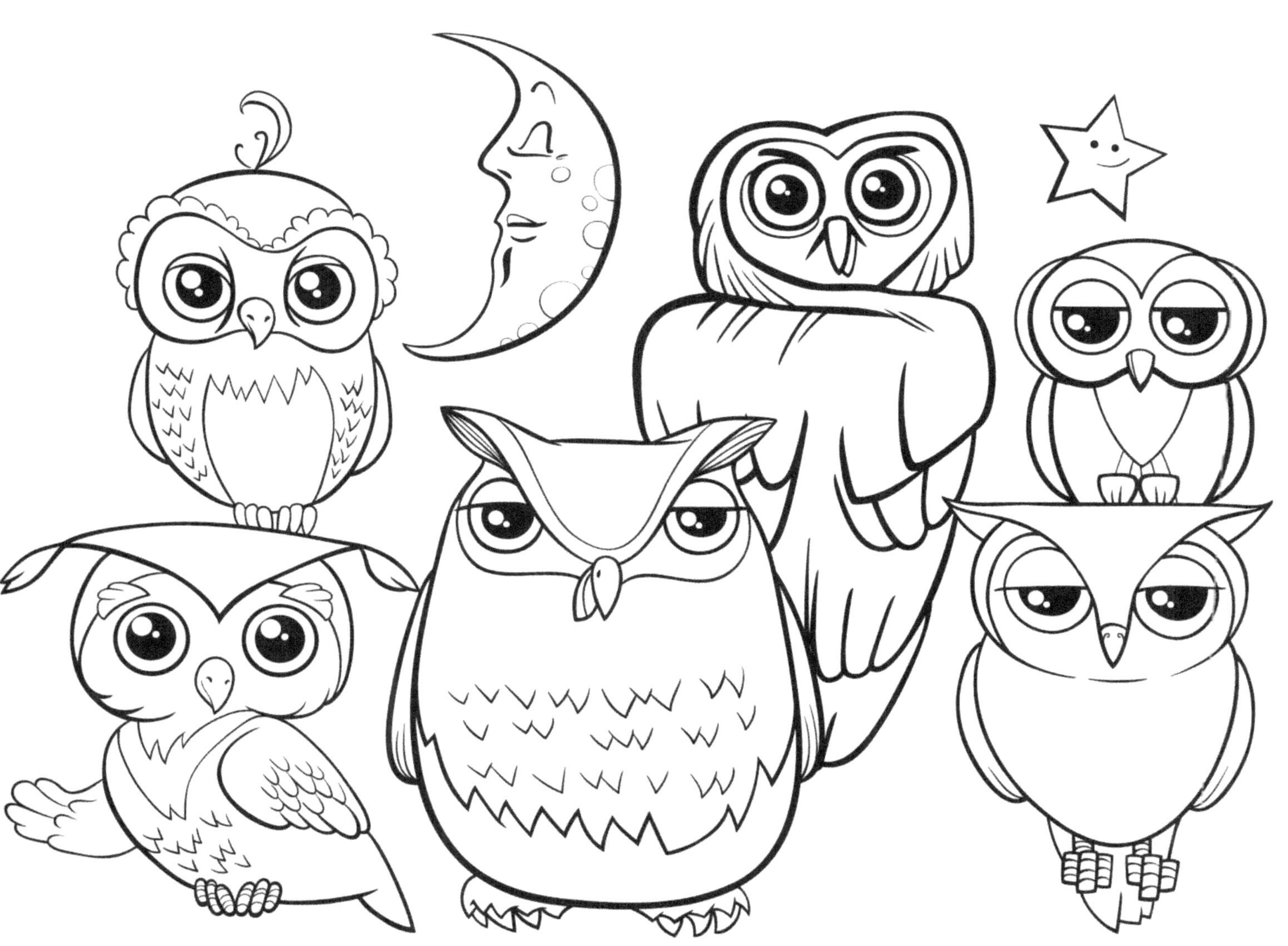

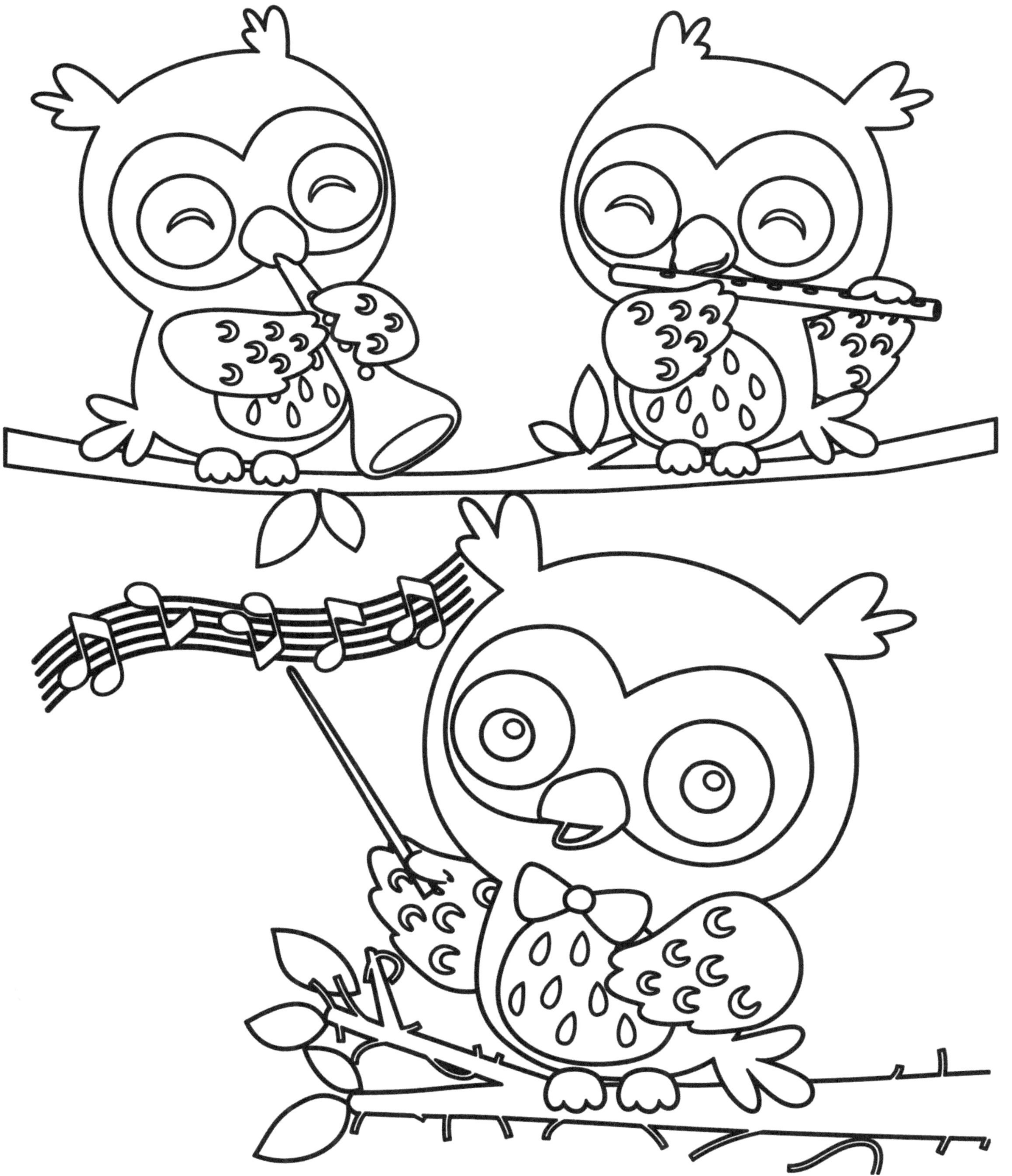

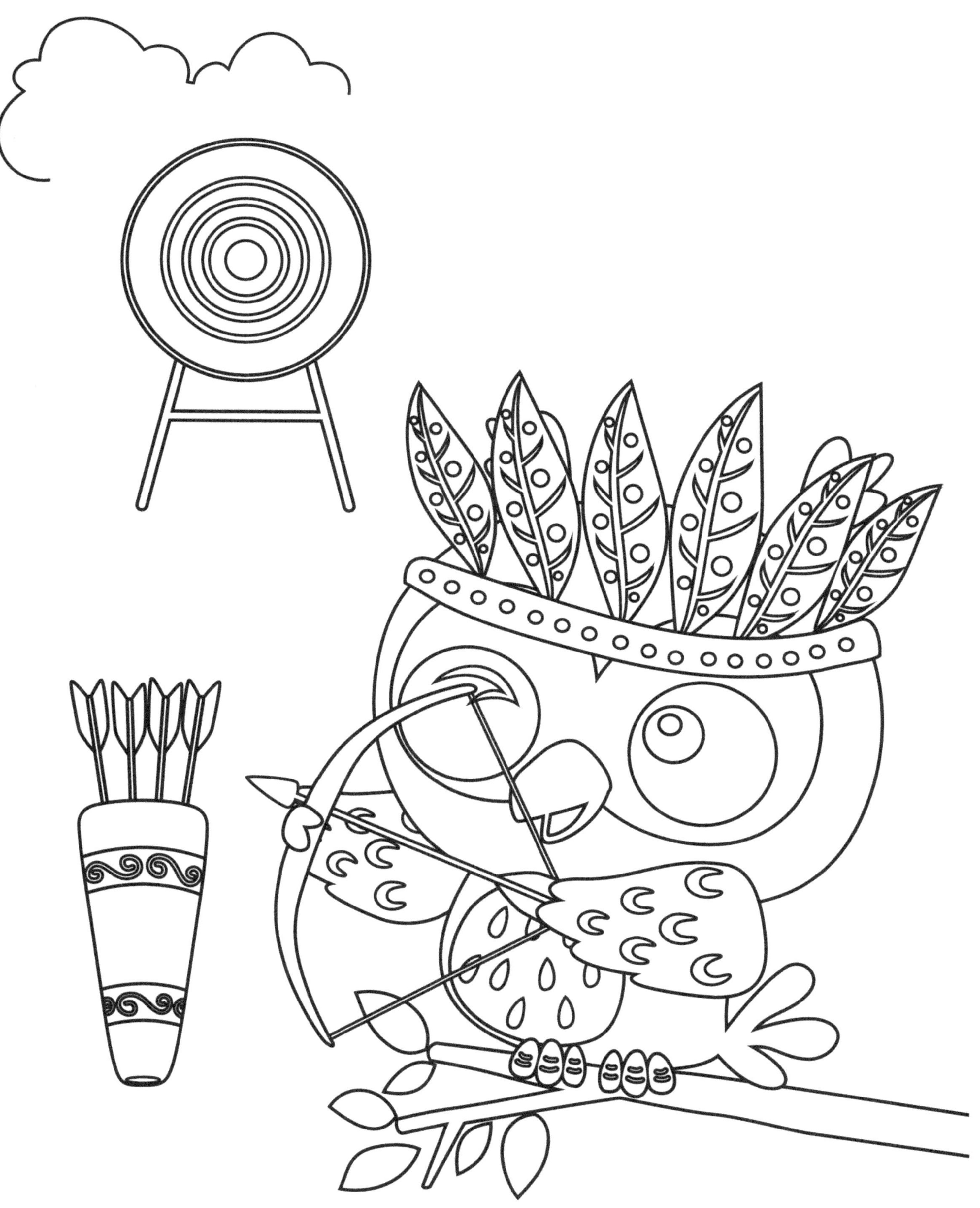

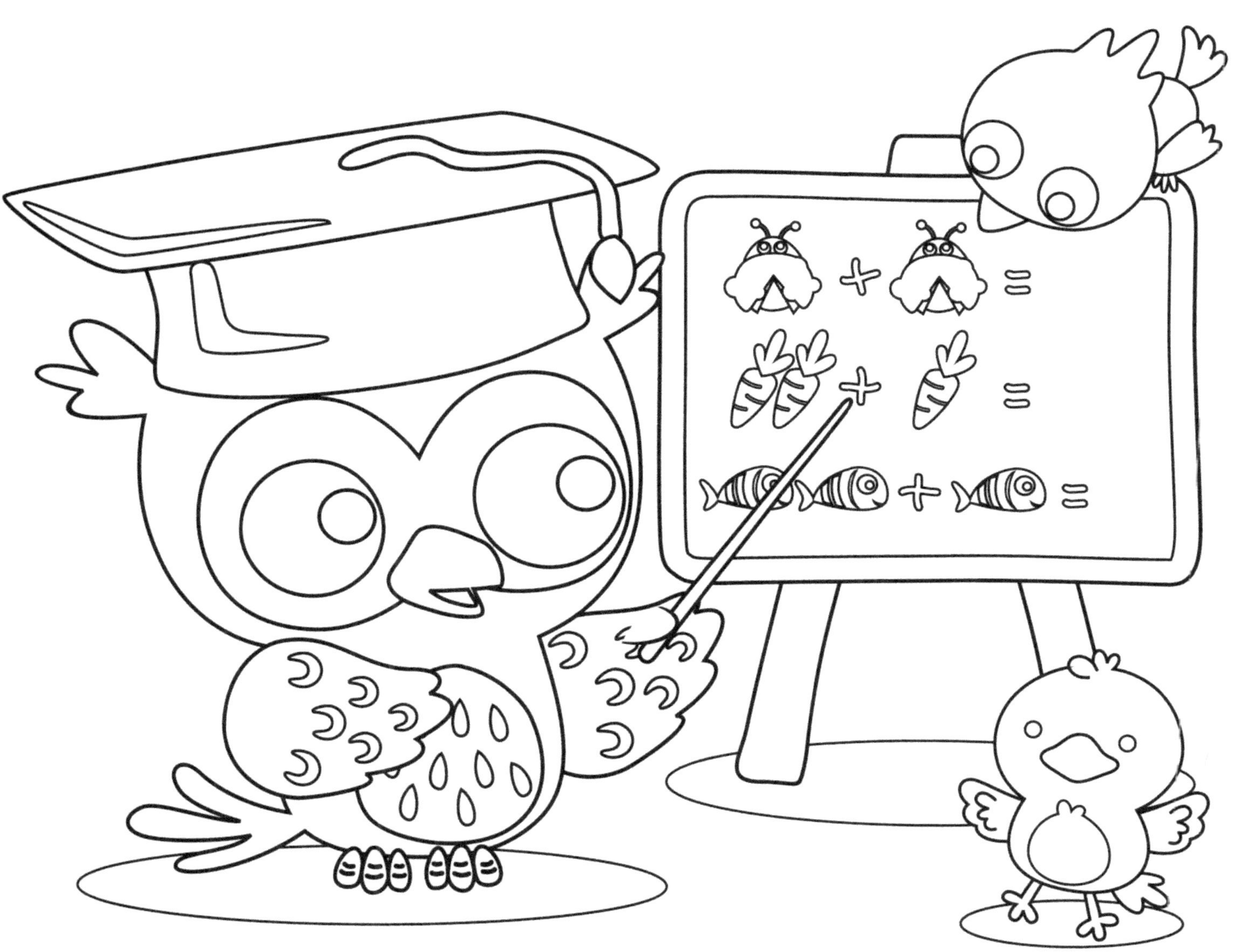